ELECTRIC LAKE

ONEONTA'S FORGOTTEN GEM

JIM LOUDON

SQUARE CIRCLE PRESS
VOORHEESVILLE, NEW YORK

Electric Lake:
Oneonta's Forgotten Gem

Published by
Square Circle Press LLC
137 Ketcham Road
Voorheesville, NY 12186
www.squarecirclepress.com

First paperback edition 2011.
Printed and bound in the United States of America on acid-free, durable paper.

ISBN 13: 978-0-9833897-1-2
ISBN 10: 0-9833897-1-3
Library of Congress Control Number: 2011924501

Publisher's Acknowledgments
The text of this book was created and formatted by Square Circle Press using OpenOffice.org, a free suite of office software. The book title and chapter subtitles are set in Latin Extra Condensed type, the book subtitle and section titles in Copperplate Gothic Bold Condensed, and the text in Garamond.

Cover design by Richard Vang, Square Circle Press, using the Corel suite of graphics software. Cover images courtesy of Jim Loudon and Greater Oneonta Historical Society.

CONTENTS

ACKNOWLEDGMENTS

I have to express my deep appreciation to Sarah Livingston at the Huntington Memorial Library in Oneonta for her assistance in locating and scanning images to develop this book; to Richard Vang of Square Circle Press for his guidance and enthusiasm; to Bob Brzozowski and the Greater Oneonta Historical Society for their assistance and promotion of the project; and a special thank you to my fiancé Josephine Tufano for typing, proof-reading, and moral support.

Jim Loudon

INTRODUCTION

Driving on I-88 east of Oneonta you might be surprised to learn that sixty years ago your car would have been under water! Indeed, the flat between exits 15 and 16 is the former bed of Electric Lake, a placid 50-acre pond that provided generations of Oneontans with the enjoyment of swimming, boating and fishing.

The lake was developed in 1898 to satisfy Oneonta's ever-growing demand for electricity, spurred on by the rapid growth of the Delaware & Hudson railroad shop facilities, in addition to the electrification of the Oneonta trolley line. In addition to its recreational function, Electric Lake provided employment during the winter months to the ice harvesters, and soon after the lake was filled the Oneonta Ice Company was incorporated on Railroad Avenue not far from the power house.

In 1954 New York State Electric and Gas discontinued operations at the Electric Lake power plant, bringing to a close a very pleasant chapter in Oneonta's history. Today nature has reclaimed much of the lake bed, while I-88 slices across the former tail race of the dam. The ghost of the lake still haunts the grounds however, through a small stream that meanders along the old channel between the sluice gates and the small lagoon adjacent to I-88.

Courtesy of Greater Oneonta Historical Society.

THE NEW
POWER PLANT

Driving west on I-88 between the Emmons and Oneonta exits you will descend a small hill and find yourself rolling along a flat plain that culminates in the exit for Route 23. At this point in your travels you are driving along the bottom of a former lake bed. Aside from a short stretch of overgrown embankment to the left of the highway there is little tangible evidence of Electric Lake, which for over half a century was Oneonta's pre-eminent destination for weekend outings and leisurely cruises.

Electric Lake was born out of a need for expanded electric generation capacity for the village of Oneonta. Electricity was introduced in 1887, with the first generating plant located in an old structure at the corner of Broad and Market Streets. The following year a brick power plant was built on Prospect Street and four steam engines capable of generating 250 horsepower were installed.

Due to rapid population growth spurred on by the burgeoning Delaware & Hudson railroad shop facilities, Oneonta continued to outgrow its supply of electricity, and it was anticipated that the city's trolley line would soon convert from horse to electric power. On March 16, 1897 Senator Brown introduced a bill in the New York State legislature to incorporate the Electric Water Power Company of Oneonta in order to satisfy the City's growing demand for electricity. The organizers of the new company were Frank D. Miller, Marquis L. Keys and George W. Lewis. The capital stock was set at $30,000 and work on the new plant was initiated in June of 1898.

Electric Lake power plant under construction in summer 1898. Courtesy of Huntington Memorial Library.

Electric Lake power plant after the installation of a steam boiler house as evidenced by the addition of a smokestack. Courtesy of Huntington Memorial Library.

The power plant was located at the junction of Conant Avenue and Factory Street, southwest of the piano factory at the foot of Rose Avenue. The crib dam at the power plant was 80 feet in length, 35 feet wide at the bottom and 16 feet at the top, flanked by massive walls of masonry on either side. The wall on the north side formed one wall of the flume and part of the power house foundation. Mud sills and planking were used as forms for the foundation of the walls, and while the lower corners were being laid centrifugal pumps were used to discharge thousands of gallons of water that gushed out from underground springs in the excavation.

The power house measured 33 by 70 feet and was erected in only two weeks. The dynamos in the plant were turned by six Holyoke turbines in the basement of the building. The wheels had a head of 14 feet and were set in pairs, with the three sets generating over 500 horsepower. Each pair of wheels had its own watertight compartment, so that the water could be drawn off for repairs without interfering with the operation of the plant.

Line shafts placed on brick and stone piers ran directly from the wheels, and the dynamos were bolted directly to these shafts. In 1899 a brick boiler house was erected adjacent to the power plant and a large steam engine was installed to augment the dynamos or replace water power in the event of an emergency. The six month construction project was supervised by Mr. A. O. Miller, who in addition to directing fifty to seventy-five men devised all the plans and surveys.

From the power plant dam the embankment extended nearly a mile to where the barrier dam crossed the Susquehanna River. The finished Lake would flood about 50 acres of farmland; its dimensions were about one mile long by one-quarter mile wide at the greatest width. The depth averaged six to eight feet, judging from the height of the berm, and the capacity was approximately 550 million gallons.

Prior to completion of the plant, the developers entered into a contract with the Oneonta Electric Light and Power Company to furnish that entity with electricity for the city's commercial and street lighting. It was estimated that this would consume about 250 horsepower, leaving 50% of the plant's capacity available for commercial purposes. On April 11, 1902 ownership of the property was legally transferred to the Oneonta Light and Power Company, and in 1918 the

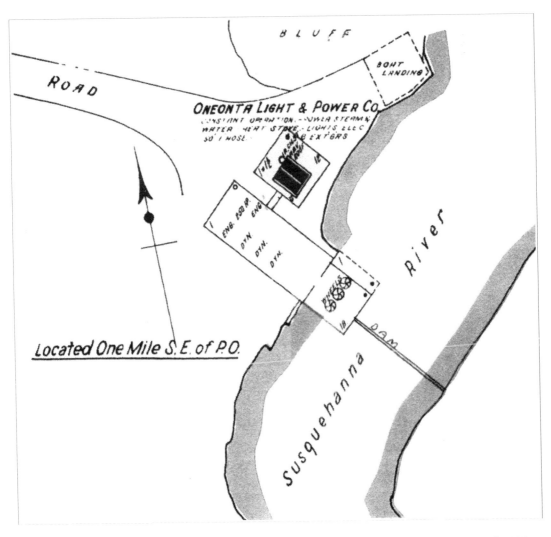

Layout of the power plant, boiler room and boat landing. Detail from the Sanborn Insurance Atlas of 1910.

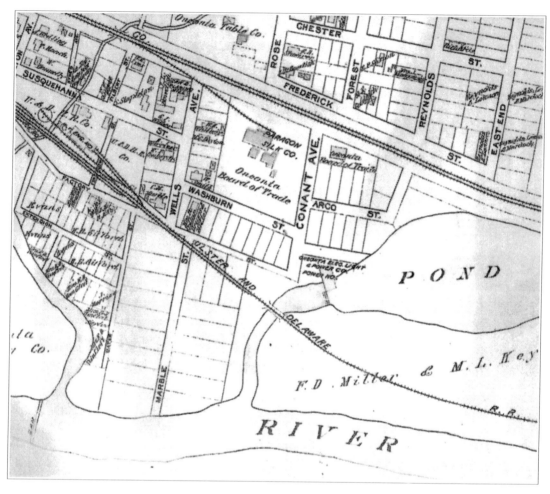

Location of Electric Lake and the power plant in relation to Oneonta. Detail from the New Century Atlas of Otsego County of 1903.

property was purchased by Associated Electric and Gas which would later become New York State Electric and Gas Corporation.

Throughout the first half of the twentieth century Electric Lake was a favorite spot for picnics, swimming and boating. There was a picnic grove and boat landing located toward the rear of the lot now owned by Otsego Iron and Metal Company. There was also a second boat dock and picnic area adjacent to the upper barrier dam. Ice skating was a popular activity in the winter months, although it was somewhat limited by the harvesting of ice which provided a substantial source of revenue for the Oneonta Ice Company whose warehouse was located just west of the Ulster & Delaware railroad depot along the mill race.

Tragedy struck Electric Lake on June 17, 1907 when a twelve-year-old boy was drowned in the plant's tail race, the only known fatality at the site. The following article from *The Oneonta Herald* of June 20, 1907 details the accident:

A sad accident occurred Monday afternoon in the tail race of the electric dam at East End, where George E., the 12-year-old son of Mr. and Mrs. A. J. Brown of Chester Avenue, was drowned while bathing. The boy, accompanied by his brother Daniel, who was one year older, was bathing in the river; and George, who was unable to swim, was soon beyond his depth. His older brother, hearing his terrified cry, went to his assistance and attempted several times to swim with him to shore. The young boy, however, was thoroughly frightened and dragged the older one down two or three times. The latter was finally obliged to give up the effort, as otherwise both would have been drowned.

He at once hurried home, while the other lads called workmen from the mill dam. All hurried to the place, but it was some time before the body was recovered. Conductor A. H. Allen finally brought it to the surface by dragging a line, to which heavy sinkers and several hooks were attached, across the pool. Dr. Olin, who was early on the scene, worked over the boy for nearly an hour, but all effort to resuscitate him proved futile. The body was removed to the home of his parents, where Coroner Brownell viewed the remains and gave a death certificate.

The unfortunate lad was a member of the Free Baptist Sunday School, a bright boy, good in his studies and well liked by all. He is survived by his parents, the brother above named and a sister of six years. The funeral mass was held Tuesday evening from the home, Rev. C. S. Pendleton officiating, and the body was taken to Lyons, where the family formerly lived, for internment.

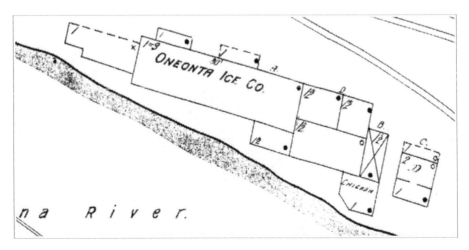

Layout of the Oneonta Ice Company building on Railroad Avenue. The company was established to harvest ice from Electric Lake. Detail from the Sanborn Insurance Atlas of 1910.

The following is an excerpt from a letter written by Duncan Tarbox to his son Charles in June 1907 which describes the drowning accident. (Letter courtesy of Geri Tarbox, granddaughter of Duncan Tarbox.)

We painted the Power Plant where the boy was drowned—I was talking with him about an hour before—he was a good little fellow. You must have seen account in the Star. I helped carry a boat from above the dam to below and done all we could to save him but he was in about 12 feet of water and quite swift and some roiley. The whole East End were there—we telephoned for a Dr. that had an auto and I guess every Dr. in O[neonta] has one. They came a doz. Men—stripped off and dove out of boats repeatedly but they could not find the poor kid. It was a sad sight to see and hear his poor mother—I think the Dr. saved her life as she was fresh from the hospital and a frail little woman. It occurred where the tail race empties into the river. The little fellow's clothes laid there on the bank where he took them off for the last time.

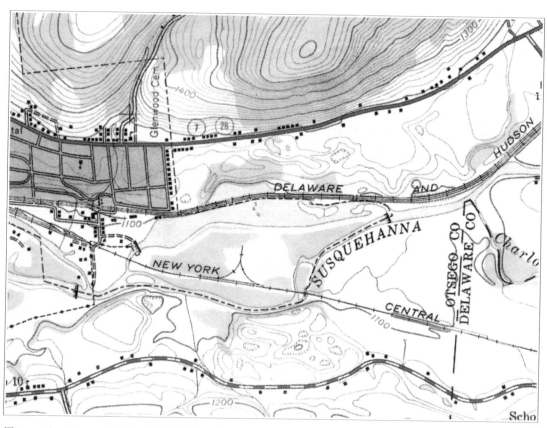

Topographical layout of Electric Lake. Detail from a United States Geological Survey map of 1943.

AN
ELECTRIC LAKE
GALLERY

THE POWER PLANT

Author's collection.

Author's collection.

THE FALLS

Courtesy of Huntington Memorial Library.

Author's collection.

THE BOAT LANDING

Author's collection.

ONEONTA, N.Y.   ELECTRIC LAKE.   George Reynolds & Son, Oneonta, N.Y.

Author's collection.

THE BOAT LANDING

Electric Lake, Oneonta, N. Y.

Author's collection.

11121. Electric Lake, Oneonta, N. Y.

Author's collection.

THE BOAT LANDING

Author's collection.

Author's collection.

THE BOAT LANDING

Author's collection.

Author's collection.

Author's collection.

THE DELAWARE & HUDSON RIGHT-OF-WAY

Author's collection.

Author's collection.

THE LAND BRIDGE

Courtesy of Huntington Memorial Library.

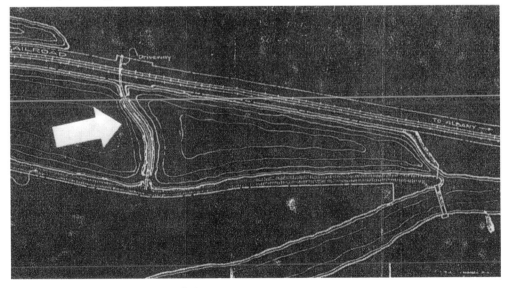

Courtesy of Huntington Memorial Library.

THE UPPER DAM

Author's collection.

Author's collection.

THE UPPER DAM & POWER PLANT

"Oneonta power house / Summer 1926"

[No caption written.]

"Bulkhead Spring 1929"

"Upper part of / Electric Lt. Pond / March 3, 1929"

The photos on this page are courtesy of Wayne Wright. The photos were taken in the 1920's by his father, Gerald S. Wright. The captions are from the notations on the photos.

THE SLUICE GATES & POWER PLANT

In September of 1939 Electric Lake was drained in order to install new sluice gates and to make necessary repairs to the turbine room. Courtesy of Huntington Memorial Library.

REVERSION
&
TRANSITION

In 1954 the New York State Electric and Gas corporation discontinued operations at the East End plant. The water wheels were dismantled and the gates removed. In 1958 the barrier dam at the north end of the lake was demolished.

The aerial photographs on this and following pages, from the GIS Clearing House, were taken over a period of sixty years and highlight the reversion of Electric Lake back to its natural state, accelerated by the invasion of the interstate highway. (I-88).

1937 - The Electric Lake reservoir shown retaining the maximum amount of water.

1960 - Electric Lake is drying up and filling in following the removal of the upper dam in 1958.

In the early 1970's the last vestiges of the lower dam and power plant were razed to make way for I-88. The construction of the interstate contributed tons of fill material to the interior of the island that was located between the Susquehanna River and Electric Lake (New Island). The fill was stored on the island and transported to the roadbed.

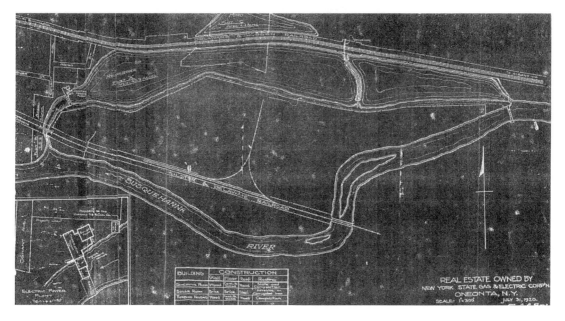

Survey map of Electric Lake prior to the construction of I-88. Courtesy of Huntington Memorial Library.

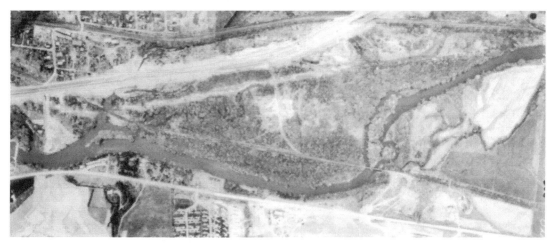

1973 - Despite being overrun by highway construction, the lake bed is showing more returning vegetation.

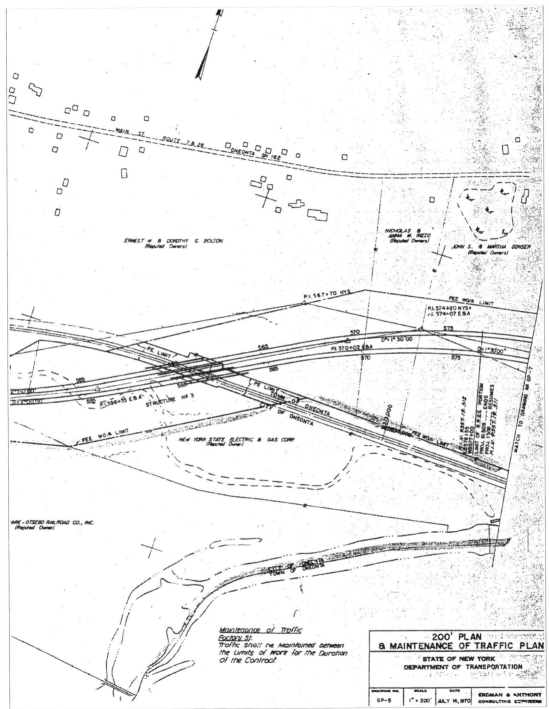

New York State Department of Transportation planning map showing the new highway slicing across the outlet of Electric Lake. Courtesy of Huntington Memorial Library.

1988 - Vegetation has returned rigorously, even after being scarred by the highway's invasion.

1998 - The natural reversion complete and I-88 firmly established, almost nothing remains of Electric Lake.

Despite suffering this complete transition, some traces of the lake are still visible; a short stretch of the old embankment can still be seen along the south side of the highway, directly across from the Delaware & Hudson Mainline which served as the northern retaining wall for the Lake. Another relic of the Lake can be found at the northern end of the dry lake bed, where the rusting sluice gates, mostly intact, stand as a silent reminder of what was once there.

Today, the State University of New York College at Oneonta is conducting extensive and active research on the greenway area now known as New Island.

ELECTRIC LAKE
MEMORIES

> *"Memory is like a treasure chest*
> *full of precious gems that no one*
> *can take away from us."*

Over a century after the gates were drawn shut and the 50-acre lake was gradually filled, it is intriguing to speculate on how the fortunes of Oneonta might have been altered if the city had possessed the foresight to preserve Electric Lake. Might Oneonta have become secondary only to Cooperstown as a destination for visitors in Central New York? Could Slade Flats, which directly abutted the lake, have been developed into a state park with camping, boating and fishing facilities? Sadly, we'll never know.

Your author has fond memories of Electric Lake, where as a boy of about five I recall fishing with my dad on the lake in a big flat-bottomed boat. My grandmother used to tell me a story that my dad almost went over the falls one time and after that never went out on the lake again.

The late Basil Anderson, a retired railroader who lived next to me on Telford Street, told an interesting tale about Electric Lake. Back in his courting days Basil liked to impress the ladies with his heroism, and he would turn an afternoon of canoeing into a real adventure: he and his date would be serenely gliding down the Susquehanna River when she would suddenly realize that he was headed straight for the falls! At just about the moment the young lady was ready to abandon ship, Basil would deftly swing the canoe through the sluice gates and onto the lake. I'm sure Basil checked to make sure the gates were open prior to his Sunday afternoon adventures.

The backwater just north of the Delaware & Hudson Mainline was known by locals as the "Horseshoe." Frank Montgomery of Davenport lived on Rose Avenue when he was a child, and recalls that he and his dad used to go fishing on this pond, which was near the land bridge that crossed to the other side of the lake.

Wayne Wright lived on Sand Street in Oneonta's East End, and recalls an incident that happened shortly after the lake was drained in 1954. A large snapping turtle that had been residing in the Lake was suddenly forced to look for a new home. The turtle

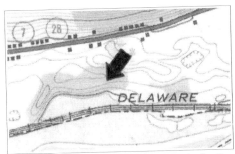

USGS topographical map, the arrow indicating the "Horseshoe."

wandered into the yard at the Wright residence, and to Wayne—who was about five at the time —the snapper seemed enormous! Wayne's grandfather, Edwin Smith, carefully picked up the turtle and placed it into their vehicle, and he and Wayne safely transported the unexpected visitor to a new home in another lake nearby.

ELECTRIC LAKE
THEN AND NOW

THE POWER PLANT AND TAIL RACE

Courtesy of Huntington Memorial Library.

View from the old Ulster & Delaware railroad trestle. Photo by the author.

THE BOAT LANDING

Author's collection.

View from the westbound lane of I-88. Photo by the author.

THE VIEW WEST TOWARD ONEONTA

Electric Lake, Oneonta, N. Y.

Author's collection.

The same view today from I-88. The image has been enhanced to try and highlight the curve of the tracks beyond the railing. (Author's note: it is not possible to take this view from exactly the same location as above, as anyone caught trespassing on railroad property faces immediate arrest.)

THE UPPER DAM

Upper Bulkhead, Susquehanna River, (Springtime), Oneonta, N. Y.

Author's collection.

Photo by the author.

VESTIGES
OF THE LAKE

The Delaware & Hudson Mainline, visible in the center of the photo, served as the north retaining wall for Electric Lake. Photo by the author.

The south retaining wall, visible in the center of the photo, adjacent to the eastbound lane of I-88. Photo by the author.

This small stream, the "ghost" of Electric Lake, still courses through the overgrown lake bed. The bank on the left drops down from the ridge that carries the Delaware & Hudson Mainline which served as the north retaining wall for the lake. Photo by the author.

The mouth of Electric Lake with the sluice gates visible in the distance. Photo by the author.

Two views of the sluice gates, lake side. Photos by the author.

Two views of the sluice gates, river side. Photos by the author.

Remains of wing wall. Photo by the author.

SOURCES

Electric Water Power Co. to Oneonta Light and Power Co., April 11, 1918. (Warranty Deed)

Fye, David. *New Island: A Landscape in Transition,* http://external.oneonta.edu/greenway/NewIslandMasterFile/greenway/GIS/index.html

Insurance Map of Oneonta, Otsego County, New York. Sanborn Map Company, 1910.

Moore, Edwin. *In Old Oneonta, Volume 1.* Oneonta: Upper Susquehanna Historical Society, 1962.

New Century Atlas of Otsego County, 1903.

Oneonta Herald, Oneonta, December 13, 1898; June 20, 1907.

Oneonta Star, September 14, 1939.

Real Estate Owned by New York State Gas and Electric Corp'n., Oneonta, N.Y., July 31, 1920. (Survey Map)

Topographical Map. United States Geological Survey, 1943.

MORE ABOUT ONEONTA'S HISTORY

The definitive account of the birth, life, and death of the world's largest railroad roundhouse, built in the early 1900s in Oneonta, New York. Describes in detail the earlier round-houses built on the site by the Delaware & Hudson Railroad, and how the company's rapid growth led to the turntable's expansion. The book is heavily illustrated, with 122 photos and 53 maps and diagrams, including full schematics for the roundhouse, turntable, and adjacent buildings. Other chapters focus on the D&H's Challenger locomotives, the coal pocket fire of 1946, photographs of the building taken only months before the remaining structure was dismantled.

ISBN# 978-0-9789066-8-9, 100 pages, 2nd edition.

Arguably the most important presence in the history of Oneonta, New York, Harvey Baker was a prolific writer who contributed to several Otsego County papers throughout his life. In 1892 and 1893, he wrote a series of sixty-three articles for the *Oneonta Herald*, his account of how Oneonta evolved from aboriginal lands to frontier settlements, a bustling village, and eventually to a railroad-ing powerhouse. This current publication of Baker's history, compiled by the Greater Oneonta Historical Society, makes it widely accessible for the first time since its initial publication more than one hundred years ago.

ISBN# 978-0-9789066-7-2, 248 pages, illustrated.

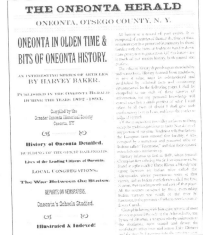

WWW.SQUARECIRCLEPRESS.COM

Breinigsville, PA USA
03 April 2011
258939BV00005BB/1/P